TURNING POINTS IN HISTORY

D1099898

The Cuban Missile Crisis

To the Brink of World War III

FERGUS FLEMING

Heinemann LIBRARY

www.heinemann.co.uk
Visit our website to find out more information about Heinemann Library books.

To order:
☎ Phone 44 (0) 1865 888066
▤ Send a fax to 44 (0) 1865 314091
▭ Visit the Heinemann Bookshop at www.heinemann.co.uk to browse our catalogue and order online.

First published in Great Britain by Heinemann Library, Halley Court, Jordan Hill, Oxford OX2 8EJ, a division of Reed Educational and Professional Publishing Ltd. Heinemann is a registered trademark of Reed Educational & Professional Publishing Limited.

OXFORD MELBOURNE AUCKLAND JOHANNESBURG BLANTYRE
GABORONE IBADAN PORTSMOUTH NH (USA) CHICAGO

© Reed Educational and Professional Publishing Ltd 2001

Produced for Heinemann Library by Discovery Books Limited
Designed by Ian Winton
Illustrations by Stefan Chabluk
Printed in Hong Kong

ISBN 0 431 06906 9 (hardback)
05 04 03 02 01
10 9 8 7 6 5 4 3 2 1

ISBN 0 431 06912 3 (paperback)
05 04 03 02
10 9 8 7 6 5 4 3 2 1

British Library Cataloguing in Publication Data

Fleming, Fergus, 1959–
The cuban missile crisis : to the brink of World War 3. - (Turning points in history)
1. Cuban Missile Crisis - 1962 - Juvenile literature
I. Title
973'.9'22

Acknowledgements
The Publishers would like to thank the following for permission to reproduce photographs:
Corbis, p. 24 and front cover (top); Corbis/Bettmann pp. 12, 14, 16, 19, 22, 25 and front cover (bottom), 29; Corbis/Everett, p. 26; Corbis/Hulton-Deutsch, pp. 5, 21; Hulton Getty, pp. 4, 8, 10, 13, 15, 18, 20, 23, 28; Peter Newark's American Pictures, p. 11; Popperfoto, pp. 7, 27; Science Museum/Science and Society Picture Library, p. 11.

Cover photographs reproduced with permission of Corbis and Corbis/Bettmann

Every effort has been made to contact copyright holders of any material reproduced in this book. Any omissions will be rectified in subsequent printings if notice is given to the Publisher.

Any words appearing in the text in bold, **like this**, are explained in the Glossary.

Contents

To the brink of war

Soviet missiles on Cuba

For fourteen days in October 1962 the world stood on the brink of destruction. The **Soviet Union** had placed **nuclear missile**s on the Caribbean island of Cuba, just 144 kilometres (90 miles) off the American coast. The United States armed forces were on full alert, poised to attack. On Cuba, meanwhile, Soviet commanders stood ready to fire the missiles if a US invasion took place. Neither side was willing to back down. Unless an agreement was reached the crisis could turn into a world war.

President Kennedy breaks the news that Soviet missiles are on Cuban soil. His live TV broadcast frightened the Western world.

Threat and counterthreat

For such a tiny island, Cuba was hugely important. Since a **revolution** in 1959 it had become the only **communist** state in the Americas. The Soviet Union saw it as a vital part of their defensive system. Always afraid of being attacked by America, the Soviets reckoned that their missiles on Cuba would strengthen their position. The Americans, on the other hand, were just as afraid of being attacked and saw the move as a threat to their own security.

Neither the US nor the Soviet Union seriously wanted to go to war. They were the two biggest nuclear powers on the globe, and they knew that if they used the weapons at their disposal the consequences would be catastrophic and might even lead to the end of human civilization. In the case of Cuba, however, it looked as if war might be the only option.

Too close for comfort

Global calamity was prevented at the last moment, when US President John F Kennedy and Soviet Premier Nikita Khrushchev made a face-saving deal. Both sides declared they had come out best but it was the US that really won, having forced the Soviets to retreat at little cost to themselves.

The Cuban Missile Crisis frightened the entire world. But how had the crisis arisen in the first place and what were its consequences?

THE NUCLEAR THREAT

Nuclear weapons are the most destructive known to humankind, creating explosions that are many times more powerful than **conventional bombs**. These explosions also spread **radiation** – invisible rays that kill people and destroy crops. In 1945, near the end of World War II, the first **atomic bombs** flattened the Japanese cities of Hiroshima and Nagasaki, killing hundreds of thousands within seconds. The first nuclear weapons could only be dropped from a plane. Then, in the 1950s, the Soviet Union built a missile capable of travelling between continents – the ICBM, or Inter-Continental Ballistic Missile. At the time of the Cuban Missile Crisis the US had many more weapons than the Soviets but it did not have anything like an ICBM.

This US missile of 1957 could be fitted with a nuclear warhead. At the time, both the USA and the Soviet Union were rushing to build bigger and better weapons.

Cold War

Mutually Assured Destruction

For 45 years, until the collapse of the **Soviet Union** in 1990, **communist** and non-communist countries viewed each other with suspicion. Military conflict was unlikely thanks to the theory of Mutually Assured Destruction – aptly abbreviated as MAD. This theory suggested that as both **NATO** and the Warsaw Pact had nuclear weapons then whoever fired the first shot would start a war which nobody could win. It would turn the USA, Europe, the Soviet Union and perhaps the whole globe into a pile of poisonous, **radioactive** rubble.

THE WORLD DIVIDED

When World War II ended in 1945, the world was split into two hostile camps. On one side were the free, **democratic** nations of Western Europe and the USA. On the other were the communist countries of Eastern Europe and the Soviet Union, controlled from Moscow. Both sides feared each other and formed defensive **alliances** against a military attack. In the East there was the Warsaw Pact and in the West there was the North Atlantic Treaty Organization (NATO).

The arms race

For this reason the USA and the Soviet Union did not declare open war. But each side hated not knowing what the other was up to. The West feared that the Soviet Union wanted to spread communism; the Soviet Union feared

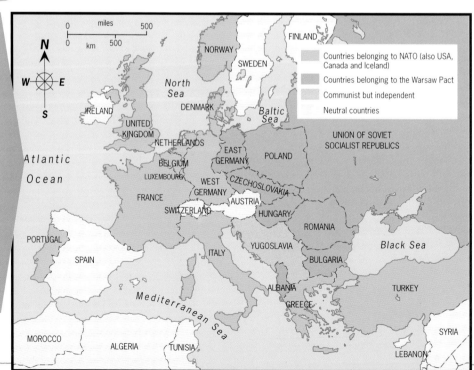

Europe during the Cuban Missile Crisis. The Cold War divided Europe into two hostile camps. On one side were the countries belonging to the Warsaw Pact and on the other the countries belonging to NATO.

that the West wanted to destroy it. Each thought that if the other side had more weapons it might be tempted to attack, despite MAD. Therefore they spent huge sums of money on a race to build bigger and better weapons, which they placed as close to the enemy as possible. Meanwhile, armies of spies worked overtime to discover what the other side was plotting. It became known as the Cold War.

The Iron Curtain

The Cold War was chilliest in Europe. The boundary between East and West was marked by heavily-guarded fences of barbed wire which ran down the borders of East Germany, Hungary, Czechoslovakia, and Yugoslavia. Berlin, the pre-war capital of Germany, was split in two by a concrete wall patrolled day and night by communist troops. The Iron Curtain, as the frontier was called, was meant to keep foreigners out of Eastern Europe and also to keep citizens in – many people did not like communism and wanted to escape to the West.

East German workers build a section of the Berlin Wall. Splitting Berlin in two, the wall was manned 24 hours a day by armed guards and was meant to stop people escaping from communist rule.

The Cold War was not only fought in Europe. NATO and the Warsaw Pact tried to make other countries come round to their way of thinking. They supported wars and **revolutions** across the world, hoping that the winners would become their allies. In 1959, when the communist leader Fidel Castro came to power in neighbouring Cuba, it seemed like America's worst nightmare was about to come true.

Kennedy and Khrushchev

World leaders

In 1962 the world's most powerful men were US President John F Kennedy and Soviet Premier Nikita Khrushchev. When the Cuban Missile Crisis arose it was down to them to solve it. They were two very different people.

Kennedy and Khrushchev, the world's two most powerful men, smile happily at a meeting in Vienna in June 1961. A year later their countries were almost at war.

Kennedy the anti-communist

Born in 1917, Kennedy was one of the youngest presidents in the history of the United States. The eldest son of a well-to-do family, he had been elected in 1961 at the age of 44. He was strongly anti-**communist** and was particularly worried by the **Soviet Union's** nuclear **arsenal**. In 1961 the Soviet Union had sent the first manned spacecraft into orbit. The US did not yet have such technology, and Kennedy knew that a rocket which could send a man into space could just as well travel from one continent to another. Instead of a human cargo it could be fitted with a nuclear warhead. To counteract this threat Kennedy pumped money into developing America's rocket systems while at the same time building more and more nuclear weapons.

THE 'RED SCARE'

Americans were strongly anti-communist. They were seriously frightened that the 'Reds', as communists were called, would take over the world. *'I'd rather be dead than Red,'* was one popular saying, as was, *'There's a Red under every bed.'* Between 1950 and 1954 a politician named Joseph McCarthy launched a vindictive campaign against any Americans suspected of being communist. Many innocent people had their careers destroyed because they were investigated by McCarthy. Other Western nations were equally frightened by the so-called 'Red Scare' but none went as far as the US in trying to root out communism.

A replica of the Soviet Union's *Sputnik* space satellite, launched in 1957. The same rockets which put *Sputnik* into orbit could also carry nuclear warheads between continents.

The balance of power

Nikita Khrushchev was a miner's son, born in 1894. He had worked as a shepherd and as a locksmith before entering politics. When he came to power in 1958 he was 62 years old. Unlike Soviet rulers before him he had no wish to destroy the West. Rather, he wanted communist states to live peacefully alongside **democratic** ones. He was worried, however, that the US had more nuclear weapons than the Soviets. He feared that if the US got too far ahead in the arms race it might be tempted to attack – no matter that the Soviets had better rockets. He was also worried by the presence of US missiles in Turkey, right on the Soviet border. In order to restore the balance of power he, like Kennedy, ordered more weapons to be built. At the same time he searched for a base from which he could threaten America, as America threatened him in Turkey. When Fidel Castro seized power in Cuba in 1959, Khrushchev saw a perfect opportunity.

Cuba and Castro

Slavery and sugar

Cuba's history was not a happy one. In 1492 Christopher Columbus claimed the island as a Spanish **colony** and for more than 300 years African slaves were shipped to Cuba where they worked, in hideous conditions, to grow and harvest timber, tobacco and sugar for the mother country. Spanish landowners, who paid their slaves nothing, grew ever wealthier. Slavery was not abolished in Cuba until 1886, by which time the majority of the population were of African descent.

The fight for independence

In 1895 Cuban revolutionaries started a war for independence, which they won in 1898 with assistance from the US. But although Cuba may have freed itself from Spain, it now found itself little more than an American colony. In theory it was a **democracy,** where everybody had a vote. But, due to rules laid down by the US, the vote was denied to Africans, women, and those who owned less than $250 - this covered all but a few people. For more than half a century it was ruled by corrupt **puppet governments**. Then in 1952 a **dictator** named General Fulgencio Batista seized outright power – backed by the US. Batista's regime was a corrupt and cruel one. As opposition to him grew, many thousands were murdered and many more injured or imprisoned.

President Batista greets supporters in 1955. His regime became corrupt and, despite his smiles, most Cubans disliked him.

By this time the US controlled most of Cuba's businesses, owned large chunks of its land and had its own naval base at the port of Guantanamo, which it held on a rent that had not changed since 1901. The US brought much-needed money to Cuba, but many Cubans disliked being controlled by a foreign power. There had already been several rebellions against US rule. In 1953 a new war for independence was started. Its leader was a man named Fidel Castro.

Castro poses with two armed supporters in 1957. Between 1953 and 1959 he waged a guerrilla war against the Batista government.

Castro the revolutionary

Born in 1926, Castro had graduated from law school in 1950 with a burning desire to reform Cuban politics and to free the island from US control. He was a **socialist** by instinct, favouring government by the people rather than by a few wealthy individuals. He tried to change matters the conventional way, by running for office. But when Batista put an end to democratic elections, this was no longer possible. He took to the hills and for seven years waged a **guerrilla war** against Batista. Castro was aided by the Argentinian **communist** revolutionary Che Guevera, who played an important part in the Cuban **revolution**. The government collapsed in 1959 leaving Castro in control of the island.

CASTRO'S WAR

Castro's guerrilla war was supported by most Cuban peasants. Seventy-five percent of farmland was owned by foreigners. Five US sugar companies controlled 2 million acres of land. Cuba's oil refineries and its electricity company were all foreign-owned. Little wonder that many Cubans wanted a change of government. Yet Cuba's more prosperous professionals saw Castro as a menace. Thousands of doctors, lawyers and businessmen fled to Florida, in the US, from where they hoped (and still hope) one day to return to their homeland.

Bay of Pigs

Castro upsets the US

One of Castro's first acts on coming to power was to **nationalize** foreign assets and to pass laws restricting the amount of land an individual could own. Americans were outraged. They were also horrified by the public execution of some of Batista's henchmen. Throughout 1960 the US paid so-called freedom fighters to bomb Cuba and to make armed invasions. At one point the **CIA** tried unsuccessfully to **assassinate** Castro by poisoning his cigars. At the same time the US refused to buy Cuban sugar and stopped trade in all but the most basic items such as food and medicine.

Castro's response was to turn to **communist** countries such as the **Soviet Union**. As a result the Soviet Union became Cuba's main trading partner providing considerable economic as well as military aid. The US was more appalled than ever. It was unthinkable that there should be a communist state in its own backyard. Castro had to be overthrown at all costs. To achieve this the US trained and armed a group of Cuban **exiles** to make a full-scale invasion.

Protesters in America march against Castro in April 1961. In the United States he was unpopular because he was a communist and because he had taken property in Cuba away from many American people.

The invasion fiasco

On 17 April 1961, two US ships put ashore 1300 Cuban exiles in the *Bahia de Cochinos*, or 'Bay of Pigs'. Their plan was to march inland, gathering support as they went, and seize control of the island. It was a disaster. The men landed but the ships were sunk almost immediately by Cuba's outdated airforce. When the invaders moved inland they found that nobody wanted to join them. Soon things were going so badly that the US sent six bombers to bomb Castro's forces with **napalm** and high explosives. Four of the planes were shot down. On 19 April, after just 72 hours, the invasion came to an embarrassing end. Castro claimed outright victory, having taken more than 1000 prisoners-of-war.

Prisoners-of-war line up after the Bay of Pigs disaster. Almost all of the 1300 invaders were captured by Castro's army. Many were wealthy exiles hoping to regain property they had lost when Castro came to power. Most were released when the crisis was over, but the last one was only let out in 1986.

Castro seeks a reconciliation

Extraordinarily, after this act of aggression, Castro urged the US to establish friendly relations. There was no reason, he argued, why the two countries could not exist as neighbours. The US, however, refused. There was no way it would allow a communist country so close to its borders. Almost immediately, it launched a new wave of undercover warfare, **sabotage** and assassinations. *'Communist domination in this hemisphere can never be negotiated,'* President Kennedy told the world.

THE MONROE DOCTRINE

The US refused to accept any foreign interference in either North or South America. This policy was known as the Monroe Doctrine. Dating back to 1823 it stated:

'The American continents, by the free and independent condition which they have assumed and maintain, are henceforth not to be considered as subjects for the future colonization by any European powers….

We owe it therefore to the candour and to the amicable relations existing between the United States and those [European] powers to declare that we should consider any attempt on their part to extend their system to any portion of this hemisphere as dangerous to our peace and safety.'

The Soviet Union was the major European power in 1961.

Build up

The new regime

Ordinary people in Castro's Cuba were doing well. More people than ever before could read and write. A nationwide campaign against dangerous diseases such as diphtheria, tetanus and whooping cough had made the population healthier. Everybody was better educated and, thanks to the new rules governing land ownership, everyone had a chance to work their own farms. The only thing that stopped Cuba succeeding as Castro wanted it to, was America's trade **embargo** – that, and the threat of invasion.

Castro had every reason to fear an invasion by US forces. He appealed to the United Nations, but the majority of its members dared not support Cuba against the US. He therefore had little choice but to look to the **Soviet Union** for help. Nikita Khrushchev was only too pleased to be of assistance.

Photographs from US spy planes showed exactly what the Soviets were doing on Cuba. They picked out the launch sites and could even tell which type of missiles were being used.

CHERRY PICKER

LAUNCH PAD WITH ERECTOR

LAUNCH PAD WITH ERECTOR

MISSILE READY BLDGS

OXIDIZER VEHICLES

FUELING VEHICLES

Spying on Cuba

Khrushchev was happy to help Castro for political reasons. He was pleased to see that Cuba was on its way to becoming a **communist** state along Soviet lines. But he also had Soviet military needs in mind. **NATO** had **nuclear missiles** in Turkey, some 256 kilometres (160 miles) from Soviet territory. In Khrushchev's view, Cuba was the perfect opportunity for a bit of tit-for-tat.

Soviet ships slipped quietly into Cuban ports with troops and equipment. US spy planes were a constant hazard so soldiers were ordered to dress as tourists to avoid detection. In their holds the ships contained everything that was needed for a nuclear strike against America.

On 29 August 1962, an American U-2 spy plane photographed something unusual. It looked like a missile site. On 15 October, as further photographs came in, it became obvious that nuclear weapons were being set up on Cuban soil. The clock had started ticking.

SPIES AND SPYING

The US and the Soviet Union spied on each other constantly. The US had the advantage because its high-level U-2 planes could take photographs without being attacked by Soviet fighters. On the ground the Cold War was fiercer. In Europe, spies used mini-cameras and listening devices to find out what the other side was doing. They used gas-guns, concealed in a bag of sausages and poison-darts fired from an umbrella to kill enemy agents.

President Kennedy meets the Soviet ambassador and foreign minister (plus an interpreter) in October 1962. The Soviets denied there were any missiles on Cuba.

America threatened

Generals tell Kennedy to invade

The US panicked at the thought of Soviet missiles so close to its border. Kennedy felt particularly badly betrayed because the Soviets had told him, through secret channels, that they would never put missiles on Cuba. On 16 October, he summoned a group of advisers known as EX-COMM, or the Executive Committee of the United States Security Council. Some, including President Kennedy's brother Bobby, wanted to settle the matter by peaceful discussion. Others, mostly generals, favoured an immediate air strike, followed by an invasion. Plans for an invasion were already in place. It was code-named 'Operation Mongoose'.

For the next few days Kennedy kept to his usual schedule, as if nothing had happened. It was important to keep the matter secret because if the public knew what was going on there might be a national panic. More worrying still, if the Soviets knew that the US were aware of what was happening in Cuba they might fire the missiles to prevent an invasion.

President Kennedy in conversation with his brother Bobby. Bobby Kennedy was a useful negotiator with the Soviet ambassador in Washington during the Missile Crisis.

Blockade or invasion?

Finally, EX-COMM came up with two solutions. The first was invasion. The second was a 'quarantine', or naval blockade, which would stop military supplies reaching Cuba. EX-COMM warned that Khrushchev would respond angrily to either option. On 21 October, spy planes photographed bombers and Soviet MiG fighter planes being assembled on Cuba's northern coastline.

Kennedy chose quarantine. He called it this because a blockade was an act of war under international law. Kennedy reasoned that this would give the Soviets time to think things over. At 7.00 pm on 22 October 1962 he spoke to the nation about his decision. For seventeen minutes Americans were glued to their TV sets as their president told of the danger that threatened them and of the action he intended to take. In case Khrushchev wanted to fight, US missiles were put on standby.

Cuba and the Caribbean at the time of the Missile Crisis.

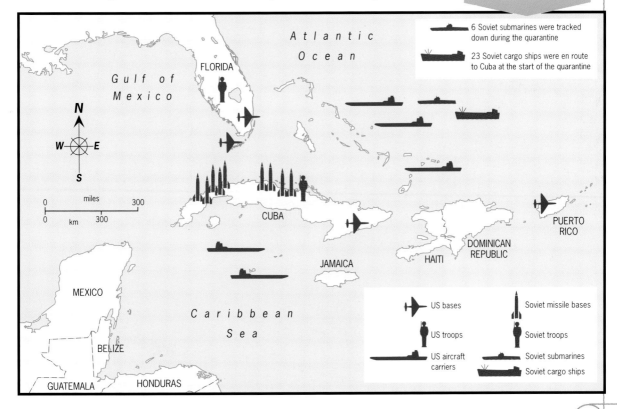

The Quarantine

Armies on standby

The quarantine came too late. There were at least twenty Soviet nuclear warheads on Cuban soil, as well as tens of thousands of Soviet troops. Castro's own army was on standby for action and a further twenty warheads were on their way.

Khrushchev was horrified by Kennedy's speech. Never imagining that the US would go to war over Cuba, he had simply ordered his ships to carry on for Havana, Cuba's capital. But now there were some 300 US Navy ships heading for Cuba. Their orders were to stop and search any vessel approaching the island. If necessary they could open fire.

Londoners protest against the Cuban Missile Crisis. It was widely feared that events in Cuba would bring the whole world to a state of war.

Two days after Kennedy's announcement, Castro wrote to Khrushchev that under no circumstances should the US be allowed to fire the first nuclear weapon in the event of an invasion. Khrushchev warned Kennedy that the missiles were there solely for defensive purposes and that any invasion would present *'a serious threat to the peace and security of peoples',* – by which he meant war. *'You have thrown down the gauntlet,'* he declared.

Eyeball to eyeball

Khrushchev did, however, tell his captains to retreat. The quarantine came into force at 10.00 am on 24 October. The first Soviet ships were drawing near and the US feared they would have to open fire. Because communications were so slow, they had no way of knowing whether the ships' captains had received any orders from their superiors in Moscow. To make matters worse, the ships were being shadowed by Soviet nuclear submarines. Finally, at 10.25 am, the Soviet ships turned back.

Open conflict had been avoided - but only just. *'We were eyeball to eyeball,'* said US Secretary of State Dean Rusk, *'and the other guy just blinked'.*

Soviet nuclear submarines shadowed Soviet freighters heading for Cuba. Their presence made the crisis even more explosive.

Trouble in the air

Full alert

The nightmare was not over yet. On 24 October American forces were ordered to DEFCON 2, the highest state of military alert in US history. This meant that they could attack Cuba or the **Soviet Union** at a moment's notice.

The Americans had good cause to be worried. By this stage spy planes were flying over Cuba twice a day at heights of only 100 metres (350 feet). On the same day that US forces were put on full alert, one pilot reported that a missile was being tested for launching. As he said, *'When you can almost see the writing on the side of the missiles then you really know what you've got'.*

U-2 spy planes such as this gave the first sign that the Soviets were building missiles on Cuba. Later on, low-level 'Crusader' jets provided more detailed photographs.

A compromise

During the early stages of the crisis, messages flew back and forth between Washington and Moscow. Khrushchev tried to bluff it out, thinking that the US would never carry out its threats. But once the quarantine was in place he began to have doubts. On 26 October he offered to remove the Cuban missiles if the US promised not to invade.

Spy plane shot down

The crunch came on the 27th, when a US spy plane was shot down by a Soviet ground-to-air missile and its pilot was killed. Afterwards, US spy planes were greeted by a hail of riflefire and anti-aircraft shells fired by jittery Cuban soldiers. Another plane was damaged but the pilot was able to make his way home.

Cuban soldiers man an anti-aircraft gun. Although their equipment was old-fashioned, the Cubans managed to bring down several US planes.

Moscow claimed that the officer who fired the ground-to-air missile had acted without orders. This made the situation even more dangerous - if Soviet commanders in Cuba could do what they wanted then no amount of high-level **diplomacy** would solve the crisis.

Another narrow escape

That same day, another American pilot narrowly escaped death. He had taken off from Alaska and had accidentally flown over Soviet territory. As soon as his plane was detected by **radar**, Soviet fighters were sent after it. The man realized his mistake and changed course for Alaska just before the fighters caught up with him. US bombers were ready to retaliate if the plane was shot down. It was a close shave.

The incident put both sides' air forces on full alert. Their planes were armed with nuclear bombs. The world teetered on the edge of a catastrophic war.

Escalation

Khrushchev raises the stakes

Kennedy and his advisers were still mulling over Khrushchev's message on 27 October when the US spy plane was shot down over Cuba. Sensing that he now had the advantage, Khrushchev raised the stakes. In a second message he demanded that the US also remove its missiles from Turkey.

The remains of a US spy plane shot down over Cuba. The pilot was killed.

World peace threatened

It had been hoped that the Cuban crisis could be resolved as a local difficulty. But now Khrushchev had linked it to the Cold War struggle in Europe. If the US removed its missiles from Turkey, it might undermine the whole of **NATO**. This made it even more difficult to find a solution.

SLOW COMMUNICATIONS

Communications between Washington and Moscow were pitifully slow. Khrushchev and Kennedy were not linked by phone, fax or email. Instead they wrote letters. Even using the fastest jets it could take seven hours for Khrushchev to receive a letter from Kennedy. Once he did receive it, he might spend hours deciding how to reply. Normally this time-lag was acceptable. During the crisis, however, the slightest delay could mean the difference between peace and war.

One way out would have been to discuss matters at the United Nations. But that had already proved useless. Despite constant pleas from Castro, many nations approved of US action. When asked about their missiles, at a UN conference on 25 October, the Soviets simply refused to answer.

Something had to be done - and fast. There was always the danger that Soviet commanders on Cuba might take matters into their own hands. Without orders from Moscow they could fire their **nuclear missiles** with the same ease as they had shot down the US spy plane. As the minutes ticked by, the world held its breath.

Cuba protested continually at the United Nations, but nothing was done to stop US interference in Cuban affairs. America's actions were approved by 50 to 11 - although 39 countries refused to vote.

The solution

A way out

America chose the simplest way out. Ignoring Khrushchev's second letter, Kennedy replied to his first. He agreed not to invade Cuba if the Soviets withdrew their men and their missiles. Speed was now so important that he did not bother with letters but broadcast his decision on public radio, which the Soviets were bound to pick up.

President Kennedy inspects his men and equipment. At the height of the crisis US missiles were on constant standby.

In case this didn't work, Kennedy drew up plans to remove the US missiles from Turkey. What he never admitted to the **Soviet Union** was that these missiles were old and due to be scrapped anyway.

All they could do now was hope that Khrushchev accepted. *'It was a hope, not an expectation,'* Bobby Kennedy explained. In fact, his expectation was that the two sides would be at war the next day.

Agreement

On 28 October Khrushchev agreed to the terms, and like Kennedy he announced his decision on the radio. Some US generals thought it was a trick to buy time and suggested they bomb Cuba anyway. Fortunately, Kennedy realized Khrushchev's message was genuine and quickly broadcast his acceptance. After fourteen nail-biting days, the crisis was finally over.

But it was not until 21 November, when the Soviet missiles had been shipped out of Cuba, carefully stacked on deck so that US pilots could count them from the air, and the Soviet bombers were being **dismantled**, that Kennedy finally lowered the alert from DEFCON 2 to DEFCON 4.

EXTRACT FROM KENNEDY'S LETTER TO KRUSHCHEV

'I have read your letter of October 26th with great care and welcomed the statement of your desire to seek a prompt solution to the problem. The first thing that needs to be done, however, is for work to cease on offensive missile bases in Cuba....

I would like to say again that the United States is very much interested in reducing tensions and halting the arms race....'

A US Navy vessel steams alongside a Soviet freighter leaving Cuba. The dismantled missiles are clearly visible on deck.

What if?

Invasion

What if Khrushchev had not backed down? In that case the US would have had no choice but to invade. Its plans had already been worked out. US **intelligence** reckoned that there were 10,000 Soviet troops on Cuba and perhaps 100,000 men under Castro's control. The US therefore intended to fly a massive 1080 air strikes to weaken Cuban defences for an **amphibious invasion** by 180,000 soldiers.

Had America gone ahead it would have had a nasty surprise. The Soviets had not 10,000 but over 40,000 men on Cuba. In addition, Castro's army numbered 270,000 instead of 100,000. On top of this, there were the Soviet **nuclear missiles**. The US assumed they were all long-range. In fact, a number were for short-range battlefield use and their commanders had been authorized to use them without asking permission from Moscow.

Throughout the sixties the threat of nuclear war was always in the air. In a 1965 film, *Dr Strangelove*, Peter Sellers (right) played a mad scientist determined to drop nuclear weapons on Russia. The film made fun of a world that many thought had gone mad.

A world disaster

Any invasion would have been a disaster. The fighting would have been hard and bloody. America would have had to send in more troops and more planes.

The outnumbered defenders would then have been left with no choice but to use their battlefield nuclear weapons.

Once the first nuclear missile had been launched, America would then have **retaliated** by firing its own. For fear of killing its own men it would have fired them not at Cuba but at Soviet territory. The Soviets would have responded by launching their own missiles against America. This would have led to the very situation both sides hoped to avoid – MAD, Mutually Assured Destruction.

A nuclear bomb shelter for the home. First sold in America in 1961, it could sleep a family of six. Throughout the US, people were afraid of a nuclear attack.

CASTRO LOSES OUT

Castro felt betrayed by Khrushchev's decision. He tried unsuccessfully to halt the removal of missiles and insisted the Americans accept a number of other conditions. Among them were:

- An end to the trade war against Cuba
- An end to undercover **sabotage** operations
- An end to reconnaissance missions in Cuban air and sea space
- The evacuation of the US naval base in Guantanamo.

America said no to all of them.

Back from the brink

Kennedy assassination

Kennedy and Khrushchev, the world's two most powerful leaders, had the closest relationship of any US and Soviet leaders since the Cold War started. But neither survived in power long enough to develop that relationship. Kennedy was **assassinated** in November 1963, and in 1964 Khrushchev was thrown out by hardliners who saw his back-down over Cuba as a dangerous sign of weakness. Castro, meanwhile, was left fuming in the background. Although the crisis was over, the US still refused to trade with Cuba, leaving it an impoverished island dependent on an increasingly penniless **Soviet Union**.

The Hotline

But something had been learned. According to one of Kennedy's advisers, *'Having come so close to the edge, we must make it our business not to pass this way again'*. Nine months after the end of the Cuban Missile Crisis, the US and the Soviet Union agreed to stop testing nuclear weapons in the atmosphere. They also realized how dangerous poor communications were.

The arms race of the Cold War had many opponents. Here anti-nuclear protesters demonstrate in London's Trafalgar Square.

At the height of the crisis, if either Kennedy or Khrushchev had responded by letter instead of broadcasting their replies over public radio the delay might have been fatal. As a result the two superpowers installed a telephone hotline in August 1963 so that their leaders could discuss problems before they reached a dangerous level.

Both sides continued to distrust each other. Each feared the other might gain an advantage and so the nuclear arms race carried on. But Cuba had taught them the need for caution. It was the nearest the world has ever come to destruction. Although there have been other emergencies since, none has been as scary as the Cuban Missile Crisis.

Ronald Reagan and Mikhail Gorbachev sign an anti-nuclear treaty in December 1987. This was one of the major steps towards ending the arms race.

END OF THE COLD WAR

The Soviet Union collapsed in 1990. By that time, however, it had made several important agreements with the US aimed at stopping the arms race. Among them were the Strategic Arms Limitation Talks (SALT) of 1969 and 1972. Then, in 1987, US President Ronald Reagan and Mikhail Gorbachev of the Soviet Union signed an agreement to reduce in number their nuclear weapons. This led to the Strategic Arms Reduction Talks (START) of 1990. Over the next decade, as the Cold War came to an end, hundreds of **nuclear missiles** were scrapped by both sides.

Time-line

1 January 1959	Fidel Castro seizes power in Cuba
19 December 1960	Castro declares Cuba's support for the Soviet Union
3 January 1961	America cuts diplomatic relations with Cuba
12 April 1961	Kennedy promises not to use force to overthrow Castro
17 April 1961	A group of Cuban exiles, backed by the US, invades Cuba at the Bay of Pigs. It is a disaster, with more than 1000 taken prisoner.
27 July 1962	Castro announces that he has invited the Soviet Union to help defend Cuba
29 August 1962	American spy planes see signs of military activity on Cuba
15 October 1962	American spy planes confirm that missile sites are being built
17 October 1962	Kennedy's advisers press for an air strike against Cuba
22 October 1962	Kennedy tells Americans of the Cuban situation and announces a 'quarantine' (naval blockade) to prevent military supplies reaching the island
23 October 1962	Khrushchev declares the US action *a serious threat to the peace and security of peoples*
24 October 1962	The US quarantine takes effect. Soviet ships turn back at the last moment. American forces go to DEFCON 2, the highest military alert in US history.
26 October 1962	US spy planes show that work at the missile sites on Cuba is being stepped up. Khrushchev announces he will remove the weapons if America promises not to invade Cuba.
27 October 1962	A US spy plane is shot down over Cuba; another is almost intercepted by Soviet fighters near Alaska. Khrushchev changes his mind and says he will only remove the missiles if the US removes its own missiles based in Turkey.
28 October 1962	Khrushchev announces he will remove the missiles, on the understanding that America will not invade Cuba
21 November 1962	All missiles having been removed from Cuba, Soviet bombers are dismantled and shipped home. The US goes from DEFCON 2 to DEFCON 4. At last the crisis is over.

Glossary

alliance, allies	two or more countries which group together in a common cause
amphibious invasion	an attack where ships are used to land troops ashore
arsenal	a store of weapons
assassinate	to murder people deliberately for political reasons
atomic bombs	extremely powerful weapons powered by uranium and plutonium. A single A-bomb can flatten a whole city.
CIA	Central Intelligence Agency – US Government agency set up to gather information about potential enemies
colony	territory belonging to another country
communism, communist	a classless society where private ownership is banned and everything is controlled by the state. A person who believes in communism is a communist.
conventional bombs	non-nuclear bombs
democracy, democratic	a society which is run by ordinary citizens who vote their governments into power
dictator	a person who rules a country on his or her own and does not allow any opposition
diplomacy	skilful and tactful negotiations, often with people from foreign governments
dismantle	take something to pieces
embargo	an order that stops trade with another country
exiles	people who have been forced to live outside their home country
guerrilla war	a war between armed forces and the regular police and army
intelligence	secret information gathered by spies and by other means which tells one nation what another is doing
napalm	a mixture of petrol and other substances that burns fiercely and is very hard to put out
nationalize	to take a business out of private ownership and put it into public hands
NATO	North Atlanic Treaty Organization. A defensive alliance between some of the democratic countries of Europe and North America to curb Soviet aggression in Europe.
nuclear missiles	rockets which have atomic warheads
puppet government	a government that is manipulated by another country
radar	a system which uses sound-waves to detect objects at long-range which cannot be seen
radiation, radioactive	the invisible, deadly rays which are produced by a nuclear explosion. Materials that emit radiation are said to be radioactive.
retaliate	to fight back against an attack
revolution	overthrowing a government by force
sabotage	the secret destruction of buildings and machinery
socialist	a person who prefers government for the benefit of the majority of people
Soviet Union	a collection of communist countries ruled by Russia. Its capital was Moscow.

Index